Sea Shapes

VOYAGER BOOKS
HARCOURT, INC.

Orlando   Austin   New York
San Diego   Toronto   London

Suse MacDonald

Sea Shapes

First Voyager Books edition 1998
Voyager Books is a registered trademark
of Harcourt, Inc.

Library of Congress Cataloging-in-Publication Data
MacDonald, Suse.
Sea shapes/by Suse MacDonald.
p.   cm.
"Voyager Books."
ISBN 0-15-200027-5
ISBN 0-15-201700-3 pb
1. Geometry—Juvenile literature. 2. Marine fauna—
Juvenile literature. [1. Shape. 2. Marine animals.]
I. Title.
QA445.5.M32   1994
516.15—dc20   93-27957

SRQPONML

Printed in Singapore

The illustrations in this book are collage
created with Pantone paper drymounted onto
100% rag illustration board.
The display type was set in Avant Garde Book by the
Harcourt Brace & Company Photocomposition Center,
San Diego, California.
The text type was set in Franklin Gothic Medium
by Thompson Type, San Diego, California.
Color separations by Bright Arts, Ltd., Singapore
Printed and bound by Tien Wah Press, Singapore
Production supervision by Stanley Redfern and
Jane Van Gelder
Designed by Lori McThomas Buley

For my daughter Alison, with love

star

circle

semicircle

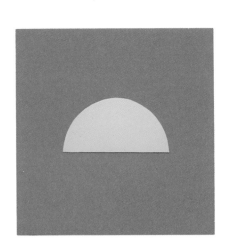  

square

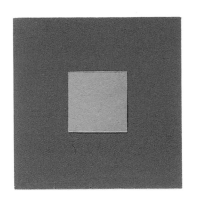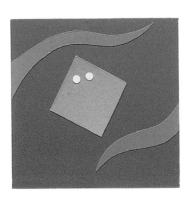

heart

triangle

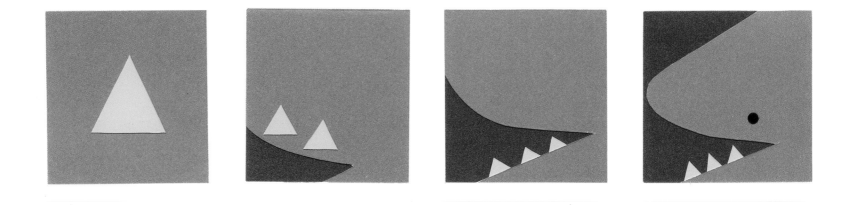

spiral

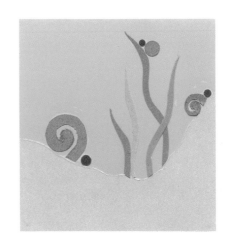

fan

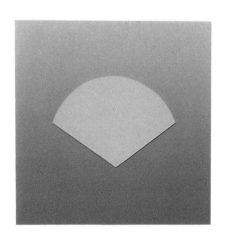  

oval

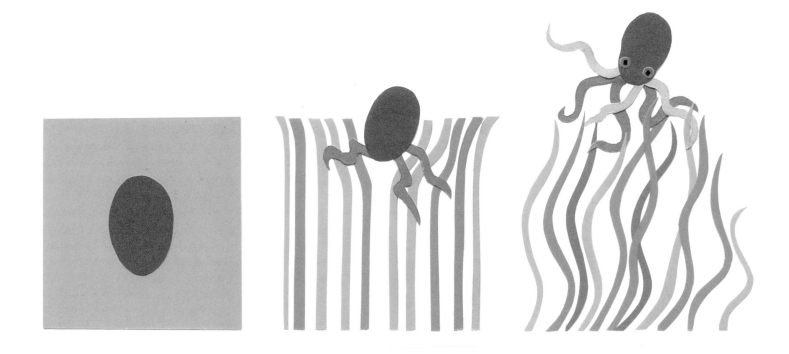

diamond

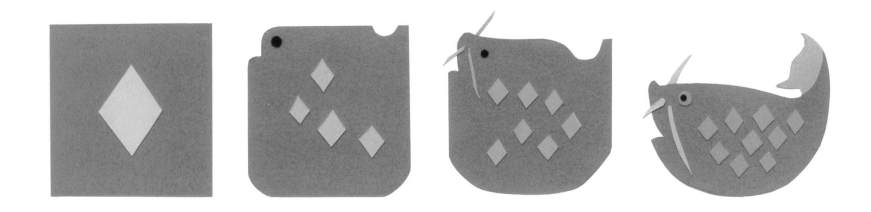

crescent

hexagon

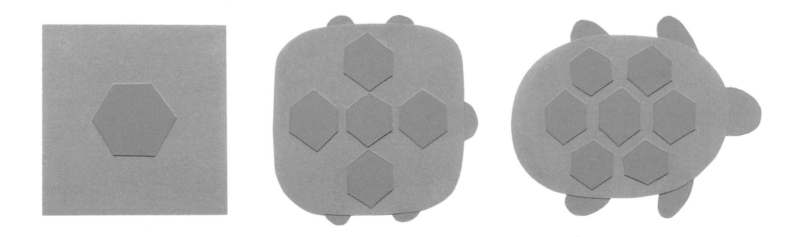

Sea Facts

Starfish can live near the shore on rocks and in tidepools or far out in the depths of the sea. The smallest are less than one inch in diameter, while others grow to over two feet. Many have five or six arms, but some have more than twenty. Hungry starfish wrap themselves around food such as mussels, clams, and oysters, slowly prying open the shells so they can eat the tender creatures inside. Sometimes a starfish loses one of its arms, but if it does, it can grow a new one.

Sperm whales live mainly in tropical seas. They grow to be sixty-five feet long and have up to two dozen teeth the size of cucumbers on each side of their lower jaws. They feed on fish, squid, and octopuses, which they trap in their teeth and gulp down without chewing. Like all whales, sperm whales are mammals, not fish. They breathe air and must hold their breath under water. When they dive, their blowholes close and stay watertight. When they surface, they blow a spout of wet, warm breath out of their blowholes.

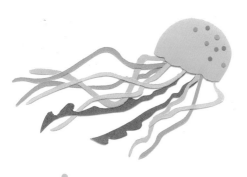

Most **jellyfish** have an umbrella-shaped top and dangling tentacles with poisonous stingers on them. Some are so small you need a microscope to see them, but others grow as large as twelve feet across and have tentacles over one hundred feet long. Larger jellyfish sting small fish and shrimp that get caught in their tentacles, then move them up to their mouths to be eaten. Jellyfish usually just drift with the current, but they can also move by forcing water through their bodies.

Skates are related to sharks. Like sharks, they have a skeleton made of cartilage. They also lack air bladders, so they must swim all the time to keep from sinking to the bottom. But skates are much more timid than sharks. They hide on the sea bottom by covering themselves with sand, leaving only their eyes exposed. They come out from hiding to eat plankton, small fish, and mollusks.

Butterfly fish have flat bodies that can move easily through the narrow spaces of the coral reefs where they live. Their pointed snouts reach into small places to find worms, crabs, and polyps to eat. Butterfly fish are so thin that it is hard to see them from the front. Some have a mark on their tails that looks like a second eye. This makes it hard for predators to guess which way a butterfly fish will swim if it is attacked.

The **great white shark** is one of the largest and most dangerous sharks. It grows to be about fifteen feet long. It eats all kinds of fish and debris as well as marine mammals. Like other sharks, great white sharks have no bones in their bodies except for their teeth. Their skeletons are made of flexible cartilage, like your nose. Like skates, great white sharks have no air bladders, so they must swim all the time. They even swim when they are sleeping.

There are many varieties of snails that come in different sizes and colors. Tropical species are the most colorful. **Sharks eye snails** live mostly in the shallow, sandy bottoms of the warmer waters of the ocean. They are about one inch in diameter and have light brown shells with blue centers that make each shell look like an eye. Although they are not very large, sharks eye snails prey upon clams, oysters, and mussels by boring a hole through the shell and eating the fleshy material inside.

A **sea fan** is a kind of soft coral that grows primarily on coral reefs in the warmer waters of the ocean. It has a flexible skeleton joined together in such a way that the currents in the ocean cause it to wave in the water. The sea fan looks like a plant but is actually a colony of animals called polyps. A polyp has a mouth in its middle with tentacles surrounding it. As the sea fan waves, the polyp's tentacles catch small drifting plants and plankton for food.

Octopuses' bodies are not very large; the biggest is only about the size of a basketball and the smallest is about the size of a golf ball. With their eight tentacles, which can be up to ten feet long, they seem larger than they are. Octopuses swim slowly, but they can hide in very small spaces and change color to blend in with their surroundings. If they are threatened by an attacking whale or shark, they will squirt ink out of their bodies and sneak away while the predator can't see.

Although most **catfish** live in freshwater lakes, some live in the ocean, primarily in the waters off South America. They grow to be about ten inches long. Catfish have long feelers around their mouths called barbels that look like cat whiskers. They use these feelers to sense their environment. Catfish eat a little bit of everything. When their barbels sense food floating by, they catch it with their mouths. Catfish also have sharp poisonous spines on their fins that protect them from any creature that might try to swallow them.

Like whales, **dolphins** are air-breathing mammals. They eat small fish, squid, and shrimp and grow to be about eight feet long. Dolphins have powerful, streamlined bodies; they can swim at speeds up to twelve miles per hour for long periods of time. By holding their breath, dolphins can dive to a depth of three hundred feet. Dolphins are very playful; when they are not looking for food they enjoy bodysurfing, diving, leaping, and sculling with their powerful tails.

Sea turtles spend most of their time in warm coastal waters where they find seaweed and other plants to eat. Some reach a weight of six hundred pounds. Despite their size, sea turtles may swim as fast as twenty miles per hour. A sea turtle can hold its breath for up to two hours underwater. When it needs protection, it pulls its head and legs inside its shell, which is actually made of its backbone and ribs grown together.